HER UNBOUNDED LEAPS

(An Inspiring Novel of Winning)

KHAGESH MAHANTA

Her "Papa" inspired her to believe that the sky is limitless. She was diagnosed with autism. But she dared to imagine her stature, where she could create music that would touch millions of hearts and be a part of the global movement helping autistic children, adolescents, and adults live the dignified lives they deserve.

Due to her strong aspirations, she let herself perspire as much as she could.

PREFACE

This is a heart-touching story of the triumph of a highly talented young lady with autism in her childhood and adolescence who overcame her situation and came up as one of the finest musicians due-to the positive approach, untiring efforts, inspiration, and guidance of her father. Her early life struggles with her emotions and the surroundings, the most creative support of her father, and her positive steps with the determination to win against all the odds, as well as the story of her achievements, are nicely penned down by the author in this book.

The readers will find out how the father of a challenging kid can become the source of inspiration and guidance in molding her life into a dignified one, full of challenges and events.

The story will inspire many people to struggle against the odds and win.

A NOTE

Just like the best seedlings are transplanted from the seedbeds to the wet paddy fields and are nurtured gently to grow, every child with autism needs to be nurtured with extreme care and love. Those children have tremendous potential and possibilities. They just need generous love and care from our hearts to grow to the unparalleled heights of accomplishment.

DEDICATED TO:

My beloved mom ("Maa") Mrs. Manomati Mahanta,

and

everyone who has been working tirelessly to help children or adults with autism or some other mental or physical issues, as well as to bring out their talents for the benefit of the world.

A CONFESSION

To write this book, I myself had to enter into the depths of the main character. I would love to remain there till the last reader has happily completed reading the book.

COPYRIGHT AND DISCLAIMER

Author & Publisher: Khagesh Mahanta.

Year of First Publishing: 2021.

Cover Design: By Khagesh Mahanta.

Book Type: Paperback.

Revision Level: 03

You can reach the author at focusactnachieve@gmail.com

This book is the result of the author's many years of observations, reviews, and analyses.

Major or minor resemblances of the story to somebody's life are coincidental and unintentional.

The purpose of this book is not only to motivate the children, adolescents, and adults with autism or similar issues to come out and do wonders through their extraordinary hidden abilities, but also to help enhance the mental strength of everyone determined to face the challenges of life and win, for the better benefits of the world.

The processes mentioned in this book are expected to bring improvements in autistic or similar behaviors unless those behaviors are caused by some physical issue.

However, neither process nor method mentioned in the book is meant for the remedy or cure of autism or similar disorders.

Also, this is for the general understanding that every autistic person is unique.

CHAPTER 1: The sky is limitless.

Like the previous ones, this news has also created a happy-jerk in my mind. However, I don't aspire to win a prestigious award like this, but am pursuing the dream of touching many hearts through my music and am happy that people have been embracing my musical tunes with great love.

I am Aarna, and have just crossed the 25th milestone of my life. I really suffered throughout my childhood and adolescence due to autism, without knowing that I was autistic. My frustration made me stronger, not to run away from the reality of life but to take up the challenges to make myself fit and capable of going ahead with my passion for music to bring peace in the hearts of people as well as work for the wellbeing of many autistic children and adults.

+++++++++

I've decided to dedicate this award to my genius papa, who not only gifted me a beautiful violin and taught me music from the very scratch, but also has been constantly motivating and guiding me to try again and again and get ahead, despite all odds. I feel, now, I am in a position to proudly represent all those autistic people who have been victimized the way I had been, by devastating teases, bullying, and negligence throughout childhood and adolescence, for no fault of their own.

+++++++++

"Aarna, let's be ready for the ceremony." My hubby, Om, is reminding me to get ready for my felicitation ceremony. He has been really taking good care of me since the time we got introduced to each other.

"I just got a call from the club office that people have started gathering at the felicitation venue."

"I am about to finish up my work, Om. Let's proceed from our Foundation Office to the Auditorium building in the next 10 minutes. Is this OK?"

"OK Aarna, I am also about to finish up."

+++++++++

Similar to the previous felicitation programs, this time also, I was given garlands, a gold-plated Award Citation, a big value check, so many promotional gift vouchers, and many other gifts.

I have made the provision that my prize money goes to our Foundation Account, similar to all the previous ones. And, in fact, 90% of the royalty earnings from my music albums and stage shows go to the Foundation Account. I have opted for both the aforesaid provisions, as lots of money is being spent and would be required to accomplish the missions of the Foundation and to go ahead, as per our vision.

+++++++++

"Your speech was an excellent one, Aarna. Everyone praised you for the content and delivery of your speech."

"Nice to hear that, Om. Nobody will believe that I am the same girl who could not utter even a single word at public places or in front of gatherings till around my 20th, even though I was always very talkative in front of my papa or while alone, in front of the life-size mirror in my room."

People say they love my music. They say my albums have helped them come out of depression and anxiety. Those compliments are the real rewards of my dedication and perseverance. But still, I do happily accept the materialistic gifts and the awards that I win and attend the felicitation events because, I feel, those will inspire the people with autism to remain happy and strive for the better. Based on the initial success that I have had so far in spreading positivity in the hearts of people through my music, I can say that others with similar childhood dilemmas can also cross their similar milestones and, rather, cross bigger milestones, far ahead of what I have set for my life.

+++++++++

Om and I met at one of my music events. He was introduced to me, and eventually, we became close friends. One of the reasons may be that, for both of us, our areas of specialization revolve around a common domain, i.e., the mind. Om is a qualified psychiatrist, whereas I am a psychologist. We got married because we both felt that, in our relationship, the required compatibility could be maintained, so that our individual goals and married life happiness could both be met. We could not find mutually compatible, better alternatives. Om keeps on saying that he loves my music and the sincerity in my work towards completion of the set goals. And, I love his dedication to such a good cause and his caring and adapting nature. We are two people with different upbringings and ambitions, but we have started a happy family and are together in peace.

I have not seen Om lose his temper, whatever the situation or status may be, because he feels that losing his temper harms him badly. Another firm belief that he possesses is that for every event or activity, good or bad, there is a positive aspect. So, it's futile to keep on losing temper over trivial things every now and then.

After ten hours of continuous work at our Foundation Office, when I sit down to prepare for a new musical tune on my violin, Om keeps on observing my movements, hours after hours. My papa used to do the same whenever he would be at home, till the time of my marriage with Om. Om takes great care to prepare and serve appropriate drinks to me, as well as ensures that the sounds of the rehearsal, even though pleasant, do not escape and disturb the neighbors. He has even made my music room sound resistant. To maintain the indoor air quality of our house, including my music room, Om has arranged beautiful gerbera daisies, peace lily, snake plant, rubber plant, and weeping fig. Every time, during the final rehearsal and also during the trial recording of each tune, I can feel the freshness of each of those plants being grown, possibly out of joy. Om has also noticed that point. At every launch event for my new music album, Om manages to stand by me.

Even after spending so many hours with me, he has been able to maintain his great participation and contribution persistently in our joint research project, along with his medical practice as a psychiatrist. I can feel the warmth of his care.

Every night, Om hugs me with his passionate love. But, even though we are married, before starting our family as a married couple, we have both decided to finish the common target of our research project that we have jointly set. Om and I both understand, agree, and are interested in maintaining this. I think the simpler we are from the inside, the easier it becomes to handle life's activities.

There are 24 hours in every day for everybody. And, by utilizing those 24 hours, many successful people have made significant contributions to their own lives, demonstrating that individual life goals and married life happiness can both be achieved concurrently.

Before his marriage, Om insisted only on physical compatibility to see whether the blood groups and the genes of both of us were compatible or favorable for a healthy baby. Apart from that, he said, the rest could all be built and matched. We discussed and debated before signing our marriage documents.

+++++++++

Last time, when I completed one long speech on my experience with the successful journey with autism, Papa kissed my forehead and said, "Proud of you, child."

"I love you so much, Papa. You have inspired me to believe that the sky is limitless." My heart reverted back to him immediately, from the inside.

It is a miracle for many, including my mom, that I have won over autism. The latest formal status of mine was declared by Om as well as by a couple of qualified doctors.

As the joint target of life, Om and I both have accepted the challenge, initiated by my papa. He formed the foundation with the name "Boundless Ambit" and decided to gift the same to both of us to work on.

CHAPTER 2: Such was my childhood!

When I was a small child, my mom used to keep me at a daycare center for the whole day as she had to go to her office. Every morning, tension started building up in my mind as I had to be away from my house for the whole day. In the morning, when the cab used to arrive at the front of our house, I started putting all my objections into mom's effort to send me to the daycare center. I would hold the door handle and the stair railings as tightly as possible and would often plead with mom not to take me to the cab. But she never used to listen to me, and along with our morning house maid, used to ruthlessly take me to the cab to hand over to the lady cab supervisor of the daycare center. I used to cry and shout without getting consoled. But my mom would simply raise both her hands and start waving at me to say good bye for the day. At that time, I did not understand how a mom could be so pitiless. However, now I understand that she did that out of compulsion.

While getting down from the cab at the daycare center, I used to obey the lady supervisor without making any noise, not because of the fact that I loved to get down. But, I was scared of the lion-sized dog, though on a rope leash, at the front gate of the center and also of the gate keeper with a peculiar mustache. The whole day, I used to keep on remembering my beautiful room, the tiny window, the singing birds sitting comfortably in the branches of the front tree, and the garden with thousands of colorful flowers. I wished to be there in my lovely little room with so many dolls. I would love to fly and swim with those dolls and cross different terrains. The fairy angels were so free and jolly. I just wanted to be with all of them. I used to miss the hills, the birds and the butterflies from the little window of my room while at the daycare center. I wanted to keep dancing, singing, and jumping a lot in front of the jumbo mirror on the dressing table inside my room.

At the center, I often remembered my papa, who used to keep on roaming on official tours for around twenty days every month. But, whenever he was at home, his presence would really make a big difference for me. Every morning, after completing his morning yoga, Papa used to play with me in my room. I would often become a princess with my dresses and fancy items, and would put rubber bands in the hair of my papa. After my hot and yummy breakfast, Papa used to take me to the daycare center in his car. I did not object because I knew that he would pick me up from the center before dusk. In the evening, he used to play with me the way I loved to. Whenever I used to paint red, blue, green, and others on his face, he used to patiently remain seated to allow me to take photos of the paint, from different angles, with his mobile phone camera. Even though he had to struggle to remove the colors of the paint from his face, he never complained about that and would later on happily keep on struggling to remove the paint.

+++++++++

At the daycare center, there happened to be so many events all day long: so many dances and songs; someone's birthday party; return gifts; cake cutting, clapping, etc. But, I was interested in enjoying myself while standing aside in a corner of the hall without getting noticed by others. I knew that I was very good at dance and music, about which my papa used to make wide compliments. Papa taught me moon walk, break dance, and modern song dance. I used to allow my papa, not even my mom, to be there, inside my room. We both used to dance with the music on. But it was so difficult to dance with others outside of our home, in a hall or on a stage, as if thousands of sharp eyes would attack me.

I used to get surprised when Papa used to describe how his friends, colleagues, and acquaintances used to yell loudly, "WOW," when he used to show the beautifully recorded videos of mine to them, in which the little child of Papa would be dancing or singing or jumping or crawling or naughtily kidding incredibly, inside her room. Especially for those who used to often observe me, they used to find my performance in my videos unbelievable.

"How can such a shy and quiet girl dance, act, and speak like a star? She may be a different girl, with a lookalike face and physique."

The majority of those in front of whom my impression was "a shy and dull girl" used to simply say that after seeing my videos.

In fact, I really wanted to play and enjoy myself with my friends at the daycare center or with a new friend. But, I did not know what had happened to me that I just could not be with my friends and the teachers. Every time, I would be back to the square as a friendless girl. My daycare teachers tried repeatedly to get me to interact with other children, but they were always unsuccessful.

Whenever there was a poem recitation competition at the daycare center or a speech competition on stage, I used to perform my best in front of my papa in the trial round, but I could not initiate anything and used to stand blank with my hands rigid and eyes on the ground at the competition venue. No word would come out of my mouth. But, I would definitely be able to recite poems loudly had my papa been my audience, sitting in the front row.

"Why is everyone not like my papa? What do people get by humiliating and making fun of others? "

I kept on asking myself and used to be disturbed. I might not stand straight. So, what went wrong with those demons that they used to laugh so loudly, making me the center of attraction? Words would not come out or would get stuck.

In the class, whenever there was a unit test in mathematics with a limited time frame to solve the most difficult questions, I usually finished up in no time, whereas others used to just finish reading the questions or surrender. But, had I ever thought of ridiculing others for their inability to work or due to a slower pace? Getting enjoyment by making fun of others is a serious disease, worse than the most dreaded diseases that I used to feel.

At the daycare center, a maid often used to dump me in a room whenever there was some party or celebration in the hall. So, events or parties would often happen at the hall without me. Why was I not allowed to stand there, leaning against the side wall and gazing at the party events?

The administrator or principal of the center would simply state that there was a possibility that many other children would follow me and refrain from participating in the party event. But the thought of the administrator or the principal madam hurt me. I really wanted to enjoy the balloons and cake cutting.

I used to badly miss my lovely papa, days and nights, at the daycare center, who used to play many roles in front of me and used to take me to the world of wonders. In fact, Papa could only understand how smart I was!

They all used to say that I did not speak at all. They all tried to make me speak, but, despite their efforts, I didn't. So many melodious songs used to keep filling up my ear drums and so many stories of angels kept on coming to my mind! I really liked to spend the cherished time I had with myself inside the most beautiful room in our house.

My daycare people used to complain to my mom, again and again, about my nature of maintaining loneliness and silence. And, my mom used to get vexed and, in turn, used to irritate me with many questions with the purpose of finding the reasons for my unusual behaviors. I used to avoid speaking to her, despite her repeated efforts, but I used to tell my papa everything, because he was the only one who had good faith in me. In fact, every day, I would be the most talkative daughter of my "good-listener" Papa.

My unusual standing pause, like a slanted statue, used to be a subject of amusement for many people, especially at the daycare center. They used to make fun of me, describing how I used to stand up with a bend towards the left. But, my papa used to describe my usual pause as a great one: "Great pause, child; you look so cute! Wait, let me take a photo."

He knew that I used to stand with a bend towards the left. But, he often tried to adjust my body slightly towards the right by gently holding my shoulder and saying, "Wow, now you look better!" He wanted me to stand straight, but, at the same time, he did not want to hurt my emotions, so he used to express his views in a great way.

I loved spending more and more time with my papa because he used to play with me whenever he could and also because he used to talk to me the way I liked.

CHAPTER 3: From Childhood to Adolescence

"Aarna, which world are you in?" My classmates from my high school often used to ask me. I often used to be there in the middle of some amazingly lovely melodies. I really lived in two worlds; one, the world I loved to dig in, and the other, the world I actually lived in. Apparently, there would be no friends around me. So, apparently, I used to stay alone. But, actually, I never felt alone. I loved to live with so many tunes that moved around me. I often used to keep on murmuring, which my mom did not like.

My papa, even though he used to keep on roaming on official works, could understand the beats of my heart and surprised me with a grand gift-a brand new violin, beautiful with an ebony fingerboard. That was my 15th birthday. My mother invited all of my classmates from our housing society, but no one showed up, not even from our tower. Probably because of the fact that my friendships with them were still at the basic level. Or, probably after hearing so many complaints from my school, my mom lost her patience and habitually spread bad about me to the moms of my friends: "I am so worried that Aarna is born abnormal." Many times, I have heard her say over the phone to her cousin's sisters, and others:

"I am thinking of taking her to a mental hospital."

"I know, she will not be able to do anything in her life and will just be our burden."

Sometimes, when she could not digest the complaints of my school teachers or the tuition teacher, she would dangerously bang her head on the wall and shout: "God, why have you sent her to our house to get harassed?"

Her head banging on the wall, even on trifle matters; shouting in a very loud voice; repetition of the same sentences, again and again, maybe twenty times; her frequent nagging, all of those became so irritating for me.

Each of the words my mom said used to pinch my heart. I used to put my palms or insert my forefingers on both ears every time she would start shouting. When discussion could be like discussion so that confidential matters could not be leaked outside the room, all the private information kept on travelling all around due to the unusual carelessness of my mom. She used to talk so loudly that I really felt ashamed and became disgusted. But, she always used to defend her behavior with this beautiful logic: "good or bad qualities that God has gifted, cannot be changed, despite all the efforts." I often had to pull her hair to make her understand that her behaviors were intolerable to me and to the people around her.

+++++++++

Even after the diagnosis of two members of our family as autistic, Papa maintained full patience and his behavior remained adaptable. So there would be no more squabbles or confusion in our family. He took the incident as a challenge to do something concrete for the benefit of the autistic people of the world. The incident that occurred in his own family made him stronger to be able to do something better instead of tumbling down.

The truth is that every time I was in a speech event during my school days, I wanted to speak in the same smart way I rehearsed in my room, but failed measurably. When I wanted to mingle with my friends, I ended up getting out of their circles.

"You are so thoughtful!" They used to say.

"You are so absent-minded!" They usually used to comment.

But, the reality was that the threads of my thoughts would often wind through my subconscious mind and take me far away. And, as soon as I came back from another world, I would hear many repeated efforts to smash my deep thoughts on life, music, pain, agony, beats, notes, tunes, rhythms, and so on. That was a high time for me and also the bare minimum I needed to possess a medium to capture my thoughts in the form of beautiful melodies before those got crushed. At that time, I could not express my exact internal state because whenever I tried to open up, there happened to be chaos all around me, sufficient to spread the wave of misunderstanding.

The obvious result was that in the same physical world, two parallel waves use to co-exist. My mom used to be very worried, frustrated, and hopeless looking at me. And at the same time, my papa used to be extremely happy to discover the depths of my creative offbeat, looking out for a suitable medium that was extremely powerful to revolutionize the inner as well as the physical world. ("rare & astonishing," as described by Papa).

+++++++++

Every child is gifted by birth. Autistic children are more gifted. Autistic adults have more possibilities and are more productive if they are suitably managed. If the flow of water is allowed to move through fertile land in a controlled way, the land will have wonderful harvests.

+++++++++

Papa himself started taking my violin classes, even though playing guitar was one of his passions, not violin. As far as I remember, for the first time, he got the chance to do his project assignment locally, continuously for a duration of six months without having to meet his usual out-of-the-station travel requirement. Incidentally, his new project got started just before my 15th birthday. So, he decided to execute his long-time plan of purchasing a violin for me, so that he could hand over the same to me as a surprise gift on my 15th birthday. During his college days, he got the chance to learn guitar from a renowned guitarist. He knew that there would be few coaches for me who would be able to teach me.

Initially, I thought that Papa was cracking a joke by saying that he would be my violin coach. But, he firmly said, "Child, it is immaterial what the instrument is; but, the concept of music is. I will teach you how to tighten the bow hair, apply rosin, do the tuning, bow gripping, holding the instrument, positioning the hands and fingers, playing the strings, notes, scales, and rhythms. But, you yourself will be the only creator of your desired musical tunes, which I am fully confident about. You can surely do it because you are very brilliant, creative, and sharp."

My papa is such an encouraging and multi-talented gentleman. He taught me the violin with great patience for six months. He thoroughly taught me all the basics in those six months. And, after that, two and a half years of full freedom to practice and development of new tunes prior to any stage show. Every time I would create something new, Papa would be near me, either physically or over online video.

+++++++++

Every mom loves her child enormously. My mom was also not an exception.

But, even after knowing that she loved me a lot, like other moms, I used to tussle with her frequently during my high school days. Because she was not ready to make some basic changes, she needed to embrace the happiness of the family. First and foremost, in every situation, she would push her mind to the most negative possible conclusion and then project that negativity onto others. Secondly, she would repeat everything many times without getting tired. Thirdly, she would keep on nagging, day and night, unnecessarily. Fourthly, she would discuss the shortcomings of every one of our family members now and then with the others, outside of our family, face-to-face or over the phone.

Giving birth and feeding milk does not necessarily make a woman a good mother. The sacrifices that she makes during her pregnancy and in raising a child are truly incredible, and there is no comparison with anything else. But, is there anybody else better than a mother to understand the child's every move and take timely action? If a lady, after giving birth to a child, cannot take the aforesaid role, then she does not deserve to call herself a good mother. I have found, "understanding" can be a major form of "love". My mom did not try to understand me. She gave more weight to the advice of my schoolteachers, neighbors, and relatives but not of mine.

+++++++++

I was emotionally tortured by everyone around me except my papa. Papa was the only one who tried to peep inside my heart and could intelligently understand how my emotional upbringing was.

CHAPTER 4: My First Stage Show

I clearly remember the evening of my first violin performance on the stage, almost three years since I started to learn. On that evening, I actually did the worst, despite the fact that I deserved to do the best. That event, however, will remain one of the most memorable in my life.

My papa tried hard to have my first stage event and succeeded in getting a popular auditorium with a capacity of 1200 people, and also managed to get 1000 genuinely interested spectators. But, on the stage, I became a "statue" 15 minutes prior to the scheduled time for the show, as I forgot everything. “I do not remember anything, Papa." I whispered in the ear of Papa.

"Don’t worry, child." He just said, whispering, with a cool gesture, even at that critical time.

With the confident gesture of my papa, I got relaxed momentarily, but got terrified imagining what would happen if I happened to be on the stage, in that situation, with some other person instead of my papa.

"Ladies and gentlemen, thanks for your gracious presence, for the show. We are going to start an exciting musical programme now, even though the scheduled artist suddenly got unwell. " He just addressed the audience and beautifully managed the situation, with great presence of mind, and started by himself smartly, in the blink of the eye. No rehearsal, no preparation; but he dared to start with his topmost confidence, to get rid of the sparks of embarrassment from the audience that otherwise could have definitely let me down very badly, inside the huge auditorium.

There was a pin-drop silence for some time, as the audience could not get any time to grasp the whole situation. But, Papa could bring the situation under his grip in no time with his amazingly good live performance, extempore!

The audience forgot that the scheduled programme they came for did not happen. Rather, they got mesmerized by the lovely tune of Papa, which was in fact new to me. He got a standing ovation from the 1000 audience in the auditorium! He not only managed but also made everyone happy and exceeded the expectations of the audience. I did not know how he could perform so brilliantly like a professional violinist.

I really got a practical on-the-stage-demo in that first show of mine, even though I measurably failed to perform myself. However, because of the brilliant stop-gap arrangement by my papa, nobody got the chance to notice that I failed to perform.

While coming back, I said, "So sorry, Papa."

But he replied, "Just cool, child. Please try to enter into the depths of your own musical tunes and remain there, so that your music can bring inner peace and relaxation to the minds of your audience. "

"This time, I somehow managed. Do well next time, child, with your own tunes. You are very creative. I know you can do it. Forget whatever happened today and start with a new promise to the world. You can do it. All the best for the next show, my dear child. "

I probably would have tumbled, had I not gotten my papa as my papa.

That event was one of the most inspiring ones for me. I decided not to let my papa down again. So, I decided to make a major change in my approach. I started doing meditation and started keeping on practicing music, hours after hours, in that meditative mode, as much as I could. During those practice sessions, I began to have ideas for tunes that would be more pleasant and soothing for all, bringing peace and repeated flows of happiness to the audience's minds.

From "forgetting everything on the stage" to "creating and developing new tunes from the heart and performing spontaneously" was a journey of six more months that included many sleepless nights.

+++++++++

Staying awake until late at night is harmful. However, when we are engaged in a work of our passion and our aspiration level is too high, I believe we are naturally active, even at mid-night. In that situation, burning a midnight candle may become a necessary joy, not a compulsion, as we enjoy the moment. I keep enjoying the midnights, chasing the lovely tunes that will bring peace and happiness to my audience's minds.

+++++++++

My papa would always be my first spectator, either onsite or online, depending upon his availability, for every new tune, I would create. He has taught me a great lesson: "Child, each of your tunes will be better connected to your audience if, while creating the same, you can connect to the mighty Nature."

I wholeheartedly follow what my papa advises. Such a person my papa is, with the most realistic approach!

+++++++++

The second stage show of mine was a grand success. Everybody in the auditorium enjoyed it with great joy. On the big stage, at the scheduled time, I entered deep into the tunes on my violin and kept on performing, to the fullest. At the end, everyone stood up and clapped. An eighteen-and-a-half year old girl, whom once her mom and many others used to look like a "mad girl", became a beloved artist to so many spectators! Then, after the end of that show, a musical album production company signed a contract with me; the first music contract I ever signed. Then the second contract came and, subsequently, so many more.

CHAPTER 5: Another Invaluable Gift from Papa

The Boundless Ambit Foundation is the brainchild of a visionary gentleman whose daughter and wife were both diagnosed as autistic. He is none other than my papa, who jumped to the conclusion of forming the foundation with the private fund he had. Many positive components that he amassed through continuous studies of human behaviors while on his frequent tours across different countries formed the basis of his foundation activities.

He is an all-time high-caliber observer who did an excellent job of noting down 1000+ keen observations on people in his diaries—some of whom he met at airports, inside flights, in train compartments, in market places he visited, in parks, in some meeting or discussion rooms, in seminars or workshops, and in many other places. His biggest advantage is that he is a team leader in an MNC and keeps travelling place after place for work related to his projects.

So many cases, from a hairline symptom that fades away to intensely visible and critical behaviors of autism and similar, were noted down by Papa in his diaries.

After my marriage to Om, Papa officially formed the foundation, including Om and me as the directors. He wished to hand over total control of the same to both of us, to which we happily agreed.

"It's amazing that you have taken such a big initiative," a journalist rightly said, while taking Papa's interview for a magazine, after he formed his foundation.

The single pack of 10 diaries, beautifully packed in a single box, tied with a long red ribbon, was another invaluable gift from my papa to both Om and I in our marriage ceremony. I consider it one of the greatest gifts that a daughter could ever receive from her papa.

Om and I have accepted the challenge of taking up extensive research work on autism that would help autistic children, adolescents, and adults have better lives and also help to raise their hidden talents for the better benefit of the world.

We both took exactly 190 days to read and understand the 10 diaries consisting of many strong cases of autism, captured by my papa.

"Every case has an ending with a positive note that can contribute greatly towards the global research on autism." This was the first comment from Om after we both completed our joint study of Papa's 10 diaries.

+++++++++

Om and I are working hard, with a lot of mental preparedness. The most difficult and time-consuming task of forming the base has already been completed by Papa. He not only noted down the cases that he observed but also wrote the suggestive recommendation for each case, using the most relevant logic.

Our research to support converting autism from the current status of "disorder" to a "disciplined order" has already started. The crux of this research project is to develop exclusive, practically verified processes for different individual cases of autism that would help autistic people go through the customized pathways to self-identify their latest distances from normal human behaviors and actions.

After thoroughly going through the diaries of Papa, we are both fully convinced that every individual autistic case is unique. So, for every individual case, our team works on the relevant pathway in the most creative way. Our team, including Om and I, do the suitable blending of the hardest and the smartest efforts to add all the components to make every programme interesting and loving, so that every participant finds the defined pathway enjoyable, on which he or she can pay full attention and grab the opportunity to discover and re-discover self. Through repeated exposure to the improvement environments while undergoing the improvement programs, the autistic people adopt new sets of behaviors far superior to their autistic behaviors. Our target is to develop the parallel mental pathways in the minds of autistic people, in which their huge energy and potential can eventually be well explored by themselves for global socio-economic, environmental, and scientific developments. An improvement programme is actually the first step towards achieving our aforesaid mission.

After going through so many cases one after the other in Papa's diaries, we both discovered a few cases similar to mine that remained throughout my childhood and adolescence. Even though my case was already a gone case due to the relentless support and efforts of my papa as well as Om, i.e., even though I have come out of the sufferings of autism by throwing away the autistic behaviors of my childhood and adolescence, one by one, in the last 5 years, I decided to participate in the improvement program, similar to those recommended by Papa in his diaries for similar cases (those he came across during some of his tours). Papa really got happy when I informed him that I had volunteered myself as the first participant in the improvement programme of our Foundation's Programs Division.

"My dear child, it's so great that you have volunteered to start the analysis of your own, in terms of the improvement of the autistic behaviors! You have set an example for all of us. All the best to you. "

Papa encouraged me prior to the start of my improvement program. Om and all the other members of the Foundation were so excited when I took my very first step in the chosen pathway of the Programs Division on the first day of my improvement program! I believe that regularly analyzing oneself is a great way to improve oneself.

My support programme was for one month at 2 hours per day. So, in that one month, every day from Monday to Sunday, I travelled on the defined pathway in the virtual reality environment for two hours.

At our foundation, every improvement session is suitably marked and the relevant banner is displayed on the concerned pathway. This practice has been continued till now and will remain so to improve the excitement and motivation level of the participants. Accordingly, my pathway on the first day was marked as "Aarna's Walk & Pause Session". On both sides of the pathway, there were live video shows on the jumbo display screens that depicted the gradual transformation from a slightly bent and unpleasant walk and standing pause to a near-to-perfect walk and the subsequent standing pause.

Had I not gone through the pathway on the first day of my improvement program, I would not have known how much my walk and the standing pause got corrected since day1. We cannot fully comprehend some facts and situations unless we delve deeply into them.

It was exciting to be a part of the team involved in designing the support programmes. I found that the programme designed for me could help me assess my improvement status in terms of autism. This could again validate that autism can be improved upon to its optimum.

During the first session, our team, including Om, observed that my walks and pauses were almost straight. However, unlike their observations, I could see slight bends towards the left side, though we're at the minimum level as compared to the clearly visible bends of my childhood and adolescence. I could make out the slight deviation by looking at the display screens.

"You walk smart and straight, and your standing pause also looks great." Om commented, to which other members agreed.

"But, Om, there is still a slight deviation that I will definitely improve during the remaining days of my program." Om nodded with a pleasant smile to express his agreement with my reply.

In all the subsequent days of my improvement program, I got the opportunity to practically see how much I have become free from the autistic behaviors of my childhood and adolescence that incited people surrounding me to bully and insult me. Just like we find it very difficult to see the backside of our own body and need to take the help of a mirror or reliable friend's eyes, similar to that, to assess the realistic status of our shortcomings or autistic behaviors, such improvement programmes are required. Similar things happened to me. Through my most sincere participation in the improvement programme designed for me at our foundation, I got the best opportunity to analyze myself for further improvement.

"So proud of you, child! You are going ahead, unstoppable. May you be blessed, my dear child. Always keep this in front of your mind: "The sky is limitless." All the best in your future endeavors."

In the official record of our foundation activities, my case has been entered as Case 1. And, since the completion of my improvement program, so many participants have walked through the specially designed pathways to bring smiles to the faces of their parents, relatives, or friends. The whole team is getting guidance from Papa's diaries while finalizing the improvement programmes for the new participants.

CHAPTER 6: From "Not being able to communicate" to "Being an excellent communicator"

Ava was a beautiful 13-year-old girl, the only child of a working couple. Like other parents, her parents also had very high expectations of her. However, communicating with others was the most difficult task for her. In school, if some of her teachers or classmates would wish her "Good Morning" or "Hey, how are you?" she would rarely reply. In the classroom, she would not talk to anyone. Whenever a teacher would ask something or make a query to understand whether she had followed the lessons or had some query, in reply to that, she would not say anything and would simply keep quiet. At the most, she would slightly nod her head.

Apart from being extremely introverted or non-communicative, she was fine in the other aspects. In the eyes of others, she was too shy, but actually, she loved talking to herself and usually would confine her communication to herself only. Only a few people knew that she had a golden voice.

Her parents brought her to our office after she was diagnosed with autism. Interestingly, her mom had already shared some videos of her creative works with us that depicted how extraordinary the talents were that she possessed.

"I was like her in my childhood and adolescence," I told her mom.

"It would be so good if, in the future, she could also become like you are today." Her mom commented.

"We are so excited to hear about your life story, Aarna! From a completely shy girl to a dynamic, excellent communicator—it's amazing! Now, we fully believe that Ava will come out of her present state soon." Ava's parents got fully charged after hearing the real story of my childhood and adolescence—how I suffered and overcame. However, even though there are similar cases, every case is unique, as every autistic person has a unique personality and so needs to be handled in a unique way, even though there is a similarity in the autistic behaviors.

A similar case was noted down by Papa in his diary number 4. As per that, we needed to collect all the information about her liking and disliking from her parents and needed to make a comprehensive list of all her liking, disliking, and the desired components. Our action-team decided to work in line with the recommendations of Papa for the similar cases that he had described in the note. His recommendation for another autistic character in his diary number 4 was applicable to Ava's case:

"Prepare the complete lists of all her likes, dislikes, and the desirable components, separately. Make use of the list of her likings to personalize her path. Then, let her travel again and again, through a pathway that is full of her liking. Then, every day, while running the improvement program, add one component from the list of the desired components, not yet included in her list of liking, and remove one component every day from the list of her liking. "

"Every day, she will adjust with a single addition from the list of the desirable components, as per her personality, and a simultaneous deduction of one added component from the list of her liking. Once she gets adjusted to one desirable component, there will be addition of one more. That process will be continued till the majority of the components from the desired list are added up in her pathway. In the whole process, the components or entities of the list of her disliking will be kept at bay."

"Superb! Let's go ahead with our work, as per Papa's recommendation! " At the initiative of Om, our action team had prepared the lists of her liking, disliking, and the desired components.

Ava's likes include: "performing moonwalk dance and self-act with multiple roles; imitating the voice of a cuckoo; eating salted & crispy fried yellow lentil, sweet semolina cake, and rice pudding; dressing up like an angel; jumping like a frog; drawing eyes and noses of girls on papers; playing the video games of car racing and taking her racing car ahead, leaving all others far behind; getting a blonde twin braid hairstyle; colorful fishes in the aquariums; rain water drops falling on the palms; and so many."

Ava's dislikes include: "bitter gourd; cockroaches; loud alarming noise from an inverter or an electric panel; lizards; nagging, and so many."

And the list of the desirable components, prepared by our team after having exclusive sessions with her and her parents, was quite comprehensive.

"Let's check whether the majority of the components from the list of her liking are properly arranged in the Communications Pathway prior to the start of Ava's Improvement Program." Om personally supervised the arrangement, as per the list.

+++++++++

Interestingly, multiple pathways have been built in the Programs Division of our Foundation Building. The Division has nine halls, each with a curvilinear pathway, to run the improvement programs.

In the Communications Pathway, there are a total of twenty-four video display jumbo screens on both sides; twelve on each side of the pathway. The halls are sound-resistant, and the sides of each hall are not transparent from the inside to avoid disturbance, so that the participants can participate in the concerned improvement programmes with full concentration. There are sufficient stands, shelves, tables, hangers, as per the needs, in each hall.

We took the ideas of halls and pathways from Papa's diaries. But, our action team members sat together and brainstormed a number of times before finalizing the decision on the sound-resistant halls and the pathways.

To design every individual improvement program, our action team members sit together and brainstorm, again and again, as and when required, so that the most optimum programme can be developed and run for every individual participant.

+++++++++

"Madam, Ms. Ava is at the reception along with her parents." The receptionist of the Foundation Office informed me through the intercom. At 11:00 am, Ava entered the Programs Divisions to start her improvement program.

She started walking down the pathway with her mom, whom she loves the most. Her own video was running at full volume and was being displayed on all the giant screens on both sides of the pathway. Initially, she tried to ignore it and went ahead, but she could not afford to ignore it for a long time. After crossing around ten steps, she started noticing the well-arranged pathway, with the majority of items she liked on both sides—sweet semolina cake and rice pudding; colorful fish in the aquariums; hangings of her own drawing sheets of girls' eyes and noses; salted & crispy fried yellow lentils in the transparent dishes; close-up video of rain drops; running video games of car racing with her favorite car that was going ahead, leaving all others far behind; her own recorded videos of moonwalk dance and self-act with multiple roles; her short play imitating the voice of a cuckoo; her favorite angel dresses; frog-jumping video; video of getting blonde twin braid hairstyle; and so many more. She really felt "wow" at the exhilarating experience in the Communications Pathway. She kept on putting steps ahead with great excitement. With every new leap on every new day of her improvement program, she developed the tendency to open up to the world with her original behavior of remaining extravagant in speech. She would take a halt to see her own actions, expressions, and words and would get astonished, again and again.

On her fourth day, everyone around her could suddenly hear her voice: "Wow, in all the videos, I am doing so well, Mammy!"

"Yes, darling. You are so talented. " Mom simply hugged Ava with a kiss on her forehead.

"For the first time, as I remember, she has expressed herself so openly outside her small room." Her mom informed me, after the completion of her pathway walk on the fourth day of her program.

By the middle of her programme, she started expressing herself beyond the limit set by her hesitation.

"See Mammy, these are so lovely!"

Every step she took used to fill her with excitement and happiness. Her layers of hesitations for speaking, smiling, mingling, and reacting started going away from her mind, one after the other.

"There must be adequate secretion of happy hormones."

"Here, she has seen many components of her liking, together, at a time. That must have caused an enormous increase in her motivation level. "

"I think she has built up her confidence in the current environment."

"I think she is fully relaxed by seeing all the interesting items together."

"Above all, she is in the best of her moods today and has forgotten how to hesitate."

"Yes, we have seen her jumping out of joy and her glossy face."

We, the members of the Foundation's Action Team, used to keep on discussing among ourselves during our daily improvement sessions at our Programs Division.

"It's so surprising to see her talking, talking, and talking enthusiastically with others at the Foundation Office and the Programs Division. Usually, that was extremely difficult for her to feel at ease and talk spontaneously with others." One fine day during her program, her mom expressed her feelings with all her excitement.

"Yes, today, for the first time, I am able to see that, since the beginning of her session, she is talking more openly with others around her, without any hesitation." I also shared my experience of Ava's progress, in conformity with what her mom had observed.

"I think she is opening up because of the availability of multiple things she likes, as well as many other things she deserves to possess, continuously for the last few days." Her mom added

Ava's mom wanted to know "how to keep her talking and smiling all the time."

"As practically, life cannot be rosy all the time, so she needs to listen to the most relevant motivational speech every day so that she can increase her adaptability to accept the fluctuations or the varied situations of life the way they come, in their own ways. So, along with her pathway walks, we have introduced a daily class for her, on attitude and other essences. " Om updated Ava's mother.

"Ava will have to come here continuously for some more days." Ava's mom nodded enthusiastically to what Om suggested. She was very happy because of the miraculous improvement in her daughter.

+++++++++

Every day, Ava would come with her mom. She would get excited by seeing a new video of herself displayed on the pathway. It was so good that she herself made her own videos at age 13 in her room and captured her private moments, demonstrating her superb abilities using her mom's mobile phone.

On every consecutive day, one item of her liking was being replaced by an essential commodity for her age that was not on her list of likings. The replacement activity was made gradual, with only one item per day. So, her mind was able to cope easily with the changes. While setting the priority for replacement, the ease of making the particular item available was given importance.

+++++++++

Ava was coming every day for one and a half months and was getting thrilled every day by the pleasant changes in the pathway. There were lots of improvements in her. Many of the essential items added to the pathway as replacements for some of her usual favorites had become new favorites for her. Prior to her improvement programme, while making the videos, she did not allow anyone to come to her room and used to do self-help by keeping the phone inclined and using her books. Her adaptability and openness had gone up smoothly with the improvement programme.

Within such a small time duration, the latent "excellent communicator" that was there inside her came out sportingly.

CHAPTER 7: From "a gloomy face" to "an ever smiling face"

It is said that smiles are positively infectious, i.e., a smiling person can bring smiles to the faces of many other people. A flower that blossoms spreads happiness with its natural jolly smile.

This case is of a 4-year-old boy who had not smiled for three and a half years. His parents brought him to our office with lots of hope.

"We have not seen him smile probably since his 1st birthday. We have tried to make him smile, but in vain. For some reason, beyond our comprehension, his natural smile had disappeared like a faded flower." Kris's mom expressed her concern while narrating about their son.

"Hello Kris, look at my face." I made my face smiling in the effort of making him smile. He looked at me, still keeping his face gloomy, which was really not matching his age. In fact, I could not exactly know whether he enjoyed my funny face, as I could not read joy in his face. The reputation of our foundation made his parents visit our office.

+++++++++

In the Programs Division, usually one programme is run at a time, so that the whole action team can focus on an individual case at a time. The research focuses on bringing improvements in the conditions of autistic children, adolescents, and adults so that a process of gradual positive changes can be established in their autistic behaviors, which in turn can help in bringing out their hidden talents and abilities.

+++++++++

The four-year-old Kris would walk with his parents every day at the Smiling Pathway of the Programs Division after the start of his

Improvement program without knowing "Why." One thing was very obvious: he enjoyed the walks, as he saw something new and interesting. With every leap on the pathway, the suspense had increased day by day in the minds of everyone present in and around the Programs Division, including his parents, as there were ample possibilities that Kris would smile at any time and his smile would appear on the big display screens.

Even in the midst of the desperation caused by Kris's autism, his parents were not able to resist their smiles at certain points along the defined pathway. Everybody present over there smiled to the fullest, except Kris.

"Our son has seen this environment for the first time." Kris's mom confessed.

"Maybe he is confused a bit by seeing everyone smiling. But, we believe he will come out of this situation very soon." I told her.

There was a positive sign on the fifth day of Kris's walks, at the pathway. He was unusually in a happy mood, even though he had not yet smiled. Smiling is the original nature of human beings. Kris's face was about to bloom, but it hadn't fully opened.

We, the members of the autism research team of the Foundation, were optimistic about bringing the natural smile to Kris in a few more days, which would surely make his lovely face lovelier. We, all the team members, had sat together a number of times and kept on dropping our individual rough ideas in the thought pool box for the brainstorming sessions. We all agreed that Papa's recommendations were not only from an observer but also from an exceptional person with unrivalled brilliance, who had already been positioned in our hearts as a genius.

"Aarna, we are happy to share with you that yesterday, during the annual celebration event at his school, we could see Kris's face brighter than we ever saw it earlier. We are able to see lots of improvements in him. We are sure to see a great smile on his face, anytime and every time he starts. " I could see the glow of happiness in the face of his mom.

"Nice to know about your positive feelings, Ma'am. Please bring Kris every day for the next 30 days, at least. We believe he deserves to have an ever-smiling face. "

"Sure, Aarna. Thank you. "

+++++++++

Kris came for 30 more days with his parents, without a gap for even a single day.

"Every day, he gets up early in the morning and wakes us up to come here. He has started to love this place. " Kris's mom told me this enthusiastically.

"So good to know about this, Ma'am. This one is a positive sign indeed. We all know that Kris will do wonders." The sentences came out of my heart naturally. Both parents were working professionals. Even though they were preoccupied with so many other activities and issues, they set priorities and kept Kris's improvement programme at the top of the list. With lots of difficulties, they were able to change their duty timing.

+++++++++

By the end of one and a half months of the improvement program, Kris's parents were too happy to see the sea changes in their beloved son, as he was no longer deprived of smiles. By repeated and regular exposure to the environment of smiling, he evolved with a magnificent smile on his face during the final 3 days of his program. The giant concave and convex mirrors put on both sides of the pathway at some portions were his favorites, where everyone was bound to smile loudly by seeing the funny faces and changed body shapes of themselves and the passersby.

CHAPTER 8: From "Having difficulty in forming meaningful sentences" to "A powerful speaker of naturally flowing sentences"

"Are you able to make something out of what he is saying?" Gunnar's mom wanted to know about her son, as she herself often made assumptions about her son's spoken sentences.

To some extent, it's OK to have disarray in spoken sentences. But, the issue of disarray to such an extent that it makes the sentences difficult to comprehend when the child's stock of vocabulary is good enough, is obviously a matter of concern for the parents of such a child.

+++++++++

The specialty of the Structure Pathway of our Programs Division is that it's like an oval-shaped big clock with 24 stations, and every spoken sentence is echoed back, in the most pleasant way. Also, based on the detailed bio of the concerned traveler of the pathway, 24 short questions and the most relevant answers would be prompted one after the other, throughout the pathway. The same set of questions would be run consecutively for two days. By the time, the concerned traveler of the Pathway would complete his or my first two days, another set of 24 short questions and the most relevant answers would be made ready by our team.

+++++++++

The arrangement of the pathway for Gunnar was made based on the recommendation note written by Papa for one similar case in his diary number 6.

Our team sat and brainstormed on the case from different angles and finally found Papa's recommendation, the best one.

Gunnar completed two months of his daily scheduled walks on the designated pathway of the Programs Division. Every day, he, along with his parents, would take a halt at each station of the pathway to view the video of the relevant question and the most relevant answer, before proceeding to the next station for the next pair of question and answer.

That practice was interesting for him, as he started to understand his own mistakes in his spoken sentences. In the 61 days of his Improvement Program, he had visited the Structure Pathway 45 times and had made halts at 1464 stations. That means he had attended the customized question-answer sessions 1464 times. Our action team members had rapidly accomplished the huge task of preparing the videos of 1464 sets of questions and answers for Gunnar. That resulted in huge improvements in his verbal delivery in terms of the correct alignment of his sentences.

By the end of his program, Gunnar could overcome many of the repeating mistakes in his spoken sentences. People could easily make out the refinement that happened in his speech.

CHAPTER 9: From "many repetitions of words and sentences" to "no repetition at all"

Lena was a 15-year-old girl with few friends. She would irritate everyone in social interactions, including the classmates in her school, due to the damn good number of repetitions of words and sentences she would make while speaking.

She came to our office with her mom and older sister. I had a half-an-hour interaction with all of the three members of her family together. Her mom and the elder sister were perfectly fine in their verbal communication. But, while interacting with Lena, I found that her speech rotated around a circle a number of times.

We have a similar case in Diary Number 3 of Papa. After discussion among the members of the action team, we decided to go with Papa's recommendation for a similar case with some customization.

+++++++++

Her usual speech during the first interaction with us was recorded, so anybody could make out how unusual her way of talking was. "Let's analyze her speech and then prepare the design and schedule for her improvement program," I told my teammates.

+++++++++

On the very first day of her improvement programme at our Programs Division, Lena reported at the reception, sharp at nine in the morning, with her mom and sister, as per our suggestion. Her recorded speech was played a number of times during her walk along the pathway. The Communications Pathway was customized for her program. The whole pathway was divided into eight divisions, each with nine stations. The number of divisions was decided on the basis of the number of repetitions in her recorded speech. There were a total of eight repetitions. From Station 1 to 2, she would listen to her recorded speech in an original way, i.e., with no cuts or editing. From Station 2 to 3, there would be a single cut of her repeated sentences and words. One new cut in every subsequent station. So, when she would reach the last station of her pathway, she would listen to her speech, with all the repetitions trimmed.

+++++++++

Lena successfully completed her 45-day schedule at the Communications Pathway without any gaps. The experience of the repetition of sentences and words got ingrained in her subconscious mind.

Every weekend, there was a new recording of her speech. And, our action team used to sit down to analyze the same thing weekly. With the reduction in the number of repetitions in her speech, the only modification done in the pathway every week was the filling up of the empty slots in the pathway caused by the reduction in the number of repetitions with her freshly recorded speech. In the final six days of her program, her speech had zero repetition as a result of the regular refinements in the previous days. So, in the final six days, the empty slots of her pathway were filled up with the best and the ideal speeches, with zero repetition of the world's best speakers.

"Thank you so much, Aarna, for your generous help! We are extremely grateful to you for solving the problem of Lena in such a nice way. I am so happy to inform that she just participated in one extempore speech competition and got the first prize. All credits go to you and your foundation team. "

Such open acknowledgments keep us elated. The whole team of our foundation works very hard and smart, with full sincerity. Every day, all the members work from 8 a.m. to 7 p.m., including lunch, tea breaks, and short warm-up breaks.

"Many, many congratulations to Lena for winning the first prize, and also to you as her mom! Keep it up.."

She nodded her head with a big smile in her face.

Every detail is planned, except the emergency situations. The good point is that every member of our foundation strives to continually develop his or her skills in communication, behavior, and fitness level, so that the autistic people of any age, as well as their guardians, visiting our office get the positive vibrations they need to start the recommended improvement programs at the Programs Division.

CHAPTER 10: From "getting mad frequently, out of very bad anger" to "showing a normal temper"

Bella was a cute girl at 14 and the apple of her parents' eyes. The casual and first-time friends often used to get impressed by her innocent look and gorgeous smile. But, her longtime friends, close relatives, and her parents knew that she could suddenly become a catastrophic cyclone that could destroy many items in the house with the possibility of injury to people staying at the spot. Within a few minutes, she would come back to normal. However, such an unfavorable incident could reoccur at any time if she encountered a similar situation or if someone reminded her of it. For example, while having dinner, her mind could silently travel to some of the previous happenings, and all of a sudden, she could walk away from the dining table after throwing her dinner dish with full force, causing an extremely undesirable scene.

With so much difficulty, her parents brought her to our office. All the qualified psychiatrists and psychologists of our foundation, including Om and I, sat and discussed repeatedly the course of action for Bella. We found a similar case in Diary Number 8 of Papa, and all the members of our team agreed to prepare the improvement plan for Bella based on Papa's recommendation.

+++++++++

In a similar case, Papa's recommendation was based on a two-option approach. He described a 12-year-old very short-tempered child who would become uncontrollably angry at the slightest deviation and would throw or hit anything in front of him in a fit of rage.

As a part of his improvement program, he would be taken to a hall with two doors inside, leading to two different chambers. One door would take him to a chamber with a kiddy punching bag kept hanging at a suitable height and so many items kept on the table and the divan. The other chamber would be with so many motivational posters on the wall, soothing music in the background, and a very comfortable sitting arrangement with soft cushioning. The hall and the two chambers would be totally free from glass or vitreous or any hard or sharp item, chemical liquid or powder, hot items, or any electrical or gas pressure hazard that could cause harm to anyone present over there. The walls, floors, and roofs of all three rooms were sufficiently cushioned. The exhaust fans for all three rooms would be on the roof and out of reach for the kid. Either of his parents or some relative or somebody else, who was at the spot when he lost his temper badly last time, would remind him about something related to one previous incident. The kid would lose his temper with the memory of that event.

For the purpose of expressing his bad temper, he would peep at both the chambers through their entry doors, as the hall would be totally empty and he would choose the chamber with the hanging punching bag and so many items. He would obviously make punches at the punching bag, in proportion to the intensity of his anger, and would habitually throw the items present in the chamber and/or hit the other items in the room, e.g. the tables and sofas that would be covered with soft cushions and kept fixed to the floor. In that process, he would release his anger and become cool.

There would be repentance in the mind of the kid when he would realize that he destroyed so many yummy cakes, chocolates, and pizzas kept inside the paper boxes in the chamber. In that state of mind, he would be taken to the chamber with soothing background music, where he would sit comfortably and enjoy a cool and calm environment for some time. After spending some time in that cool and calm environment, an interesting morale-boosting video display would be started in the same chamber and that would run for around one hour.

+++++++++

Bella's improvement programme was made ready by us, based on the idea of the similar case described by Papa, even though every case is unique. At our office chamber, Bella had lost her temper badly, a number of times on the first day and even on a subsequent day that our team managed with great difficulty.

"Her mood has been fluctuating on and off these past few days quite frequently. So, can we opt for your foundation's boarding facility for her, temporarily? We want her to be in an environment that will keep her cool all day long. "

Her parents requested me to look at her mood-swinging behaviors.

"We have recently opened our boarding facility at the Foundation Campus for the outstation kids. But, as you have requested for Bella's boarding, we have considered that a special case. In fact, we also feel that it would be better if she could stay in a cool environment continuously for some days. As a special case, Bella was accommodated in our boarding facility for one month, even though she was from the same city, at the other end of the city. Her parents were lodged at a nearby guest house.

We followed the method described by Papa. But, her stay at our boarding facility had to be extended for another two months. By the end of three months, there was some good improvement in her temper. But, even after the completion of our improvement programme, she was not totally free from her anger; the only visible difference was that the unpredictability and the high intensity of her anger had diminished considerably, and in the final week of her program, we could see her getting angry only for some valid reasons, and the intensity of the anger that she had exhibited was within a reasonable limit, unlike the previous ones. In another way, she started showing her normal temper by the end of her 61 days in our beautiful campus.

CHAPTER 11: From the "habitual repeated actions" to the "habitual controlled actions, with no repetition"

Alia was a young lady with a good interest in social science who had just turned 18. But the main reason she had been suffering and causing problems for others was her habitual repeated actions. Her boyfriend Ulhas brought her to our office, along with twenty short videos of Alia, showing the pieces of evidence of her repeated actions. In fact, she herself was aware of the inconveniences caused by her habit of repeating actions. In one video, she would stand in front of her dressing table and would do combing after combing. In another video, she would shake hands with a new acquaintance with abnormal repetition of handshaking until the latter would disengage her hand with force. In another video, while having lunch at a restaurant with her friends, she would go to the washbasin six times to wash her hands before starting her lunch, keeping her close friends waiting.

+++++++++

After a half-an-hour session with Alia and Ulhas, our team had planned a twenty-day programme at the pathway for Alia, with one short video every day, with sequential truncation of repeated activities. In that process, every day, by the time she reaches the last leap of the pathway, she would see the most truncated version of her video that would be chosen for the day, where there would be absolutely no repeated activities and it would contain only the best non-repeated activities. "Every creation becomes the best after the removal of the non-value-added portions." That strategy was recommended by my beloved Papa.

+++++++++

When the ambiance is cool and calm, you can focus on a particular event in the best possible way and achieve. Alia completed her twenty days at the pathway of the Programs Division, along with her boyfriend Ulhas, with full attention to her improvement program.

"It's so interesting to see the gradually edited versions of her videos from "so many repetitions" to "no repetition". I believe she will come up." Ulhas seemed to be happy with our hard efforts for her girlfriend. Alia used to watch each video and the gradually truncated versions with great attention and interest. Every passing day was more thrilling for her, as she was able to observe the gradual reduction of her repeated activities. Ulhas supported her and us a lot during those days, with so much patience.

"It's a great feeling to be a part of her improvement process." From time to time, Ulhas used to express his feelings about his girlfriend's progress in her improvement program. By seeing the gradual truncation of her own repeat activities, Alia's mind gradually started inclined towards non-repeated activities. While walking through the pathway, she used to observe and understand how she used to waste not only her own time and energy by habitually repeating the activities a number of times, but also the activities of many others. She started developing good sense and caution about not causing further irritations to others. My concluding interview with Alia and Ulhas was a great one. She had made lots of improvements in her behaviors and actions. The good point was that she was fully aware of the ongoing, gradual improvements in her behaviors and actions. Ulhas was the happiest person, as he had been patiently waiting for a long time to take his girlfriend out of her autistic behaviors, even though he had already become well-adjusted with her shortcomings. He was determined to adhere to her as her boyfriend without any conditions, even after knowing that she was autistic.

They met each other when they started their teenage years. When other friends went away from Alia, keeping her alone, Ulhas planned to keep on trying to find ways for her to improve. He contacted a number of places but finally decided to try our Programs Division.

CHAPTER 12: From "a kid with the ability to organize activities, but totally self-centric and rigid" to "a kid with the ability to organize activities in a team"

Nova was a 14-year-old girl with the super ability to organize activities. At her age, when kids usually need repeated pushes from behind and hand-holding support to go ahead, she developed a genuine interest and got the mastery of preparing her own plan. However, the utmost rigidity and the self-centric nature of Nova used to cause the formation of rigid mountains around her, hindering sociality. Even after having an extraordinary skill, her autistic behaviors became a matter of concern for her parents, because even after being so organized in her own activities, she was badly lagging behind in gaining ground in the required social compatibility that she really deserved.

+++++++++

After searching for a place where Nova could get the required gentle push, her parents discovered the Programs Division of our Foundation and took our prior appointment for a slot in the first half of a weekend. Nova not only beautifully managed her regular morning activities of exercising, eating a healthy breakfast, bathing, and dressing up, but she also managed to wake up her parents at the desired time and arrive at our office on time.

"Welcome to our Foundation. It's great that you managed to reach our office just in time." That was at 09:01 in the morning when I formally greeted Nova and her parents. The scheduled time was 9:00 a.m. For the first time in the history of our foundation activities, the scheduled time of a meeting with a visitor and the actual start time got matched so nicely.

"So nice of you! We could reach it on time because of Nova's plan and action." Her mom responded immediately, as a reply to my greeting. And the conversation got started.

"Superb! Thank you Nova for managing to reach on time."

"You are most welcome, Ma'am." She replied back to me, in literally no time-gap, and nodded her head with a lovely smile.

Our action team had separate discussion sessions, first with her parents, then with her, and finally a common session, including all three.

"Great to hear from you, Nova. We are all so happy to know about you! "

"Thank you so much!"

"There are big contests available with us, relevant to your expertise. Will you be interested in participating? "

"Sure. I would love to. "

"Come with me. I will explain to you how we can go ahead."

"Sure."

Nova was very prompt in giving responses. And one specialty was that she used to make notes of whatever we told her.

"It will be quite an experience for me. I can surely participate in it if I get the guidelines of the contest." Nova's assertion was encouraging not only for her parents but also for our team.

"The topic of the current week's contest is: 'Making a Plan for a Mega Group Music Event', as per the following input data:

Our input data for our first contest, where Nova participated, was:

"Contest Title: 'Plan for the Curtain-raiser Musical Concert.'

Time left in hand for the event: 35 days.

The number of participants in the concert: 24 (6 local and 18 outstation artists).

Concert location: City Club Auditorium, 2 km away from the Foundation Campus.

The planned duration of the concert: 40 minutes.

Rehearsal frequency, duration, and location: daily for 4 hours at the Foundation Auditorium.

Transportation to and from the concert location needs to be arranged.

Refreshments for the artists: Needs to be arranged.

Refreshments for the guests and the spectators need to be arranged,"

"Let Nova come to our Programs Division every weekend, continuously for 2 days, to participate in the relevant weekly contest. We have designed the contests in such a way that every participant is bound to get the practice of working in a team environment that will facilitate better communication." That was the proposal given to the parents of Nova, which they happily accepted.

For four weeks, Nova came to our Programs Division at the weekends for two days.

"Nova, let's work together and accomplish things."

"We are with you to provide the required information you need."

"We know that you can make intelligent assumptions on many matters. But let's utilize the pool of resources, ever-ready to support you from all angles, accomplishing your task."

Our action team members tried to make her at ease in the initial hours of her first contest, as she was not at all accustomed to a team environment.

But, after preparing the basic plan for the first contest she participated in, she had to communicate with the members of our action team to complete the further steps of the plan. She had to participate in the live-chats, again and again; had to talk with our team members, again and again, to get the inputs as well as to get the matters clarified; had to send and receive e-mails, a number of times; had to go through the data verification and step approval process, a number of times. In the subsequent three weeks, she had to go through the similar processes that she followed for the first contest to complete participation in another three contests.

Nova got the live practice of interacting with the relevant people in the teams to complete four consecutive entries in four contests, which were nothing but four individual Planning Sheets, complete in all the aspects. So, after four weeks, she no longer remained as a standalone planner where she would execute everything herself as per her personal perspective, by devoting odd hours of the day, even at midnight. She also got the opportunity to enhance her outstanding ability to organize multiple activities in a team environment by dedicating the limited scheduled hours so that her daily schedule of sports, exercises, late evening walks, sleep, etc. would not be hampered.

With the submission of her entry for every subsequent contest, Nova started getting more exposure to working in a healthier team environment. When the result of the 4th contest came out, she and her family members were overwhelmed with joy, as she was judged as the best contestant.

For four weeks, she was busy with the weekly contests in the team environments. For two more weeks, we conducted her daily motivational sessions and counseling on team spirit. She got a very warm felicitation for winning her 4th contest, and by dint of that win, she got the opportunity to participate in another two weekly contests, where her entries were highly appreciated by all concerned. She got the second and the first prize, respectively, in both of those. By the end of her six weeks at our foundation, she developed the ability to a considerable height as a motivated team player, with better spontaneity in organizing events.

At the end of the sixth week in our programmes division, Nova emerged as a different girl.

"Independence sounds good, but inter-dependence is far better and in fact needed for great accomplishments and sustenance." Perhaps such motivational sentences got deeply ingrained in the ears of Nova during her motivational classes, as she herself started behaving as a flexible team player.

"Thank you so much, Aarna and your team, for bringing such a dramatic change to Nova, so naturally! We are so relaxed now! We are highly obliged to you." The e-mail sent by her parents was really encouraging. Her parents were very happy, as they had understood that the social essence that she gained during her participation in the contests and the motivational classes helped her raise her unique talents for organizing events.

+++++++++

We, the members of our action team, would strive every day to arrive at the Foundation Office as early as possible, and our minds would not prepare to leave the office in the evening unless the targeted tasks were completed. "Motivate others to get better motivated" has become one of our slogans.

CHAPTER 13: From a "rowdy boy" to a "cool and composed boy"

Ryan was a very smart, dynamic, and intelligent 10-year-old. But the matter with which his parents were most concerned was the bad name "rowdy boy" that he had earned both in school and in their neighborhood. He used to quarrel with everyone; talk and shout very loudly; use very rough words and phrases; and throw the dish or the bowl if the taste of food was not up to the mark as per his needs. He often used to disobey what his parents and teachers asked or suggested to do. His parents chose to bring him to our Foundation Office. We had separate preliminary sessions with Ryan and with his parents.

"Please do something, Aarna, for our son. He lets us down every day, everywhere. We are so worried because of his behaviors and the responses! "

A healthy baby was born named Ryan 10 years ago. Initially, he learned how to cry; then, how to smile. As an infant, he was cool and lovely. Apparently, he did not carry any odd behaviors with him when taking birth. It means he had seen those behaviors in and around him or on social media and had adopted them from various sources, in varied proportions.

I tried to put the parents of Ryan at ease. Both were working in two different organizations in different domains. On the working days, when they would come back home, they would be left with no further energy to spend the required quality time with their son. Ryan would come back home from school himself, open his doors himself, change his clothes, take a bath, make the food warm, and eat lunch all by himself. After that, he would switch on his phone to enjoy action movies till his parents came back. Gradually, he adopted many fighting techniques and abusive words.

"I hope Ryan will be back to his original nature, with the required refinements. Our trainers and coaches will practically teach him moral education through a series of interesting live dramas and videos that will help him bounce out the disruptive thoughts from his mind. His daily improvement sessions will be started from the coming week onwards, for the next six months. Please manage to make him available every day for three hours for the moral study lesson from 4 pm to 7 pm." I explained the plan to his mom.

"Sure, Aarna. Thank you so much!" His parents responded quickly, despite the fact that they were too busy with their professional work to spare three hours of their day, not to mention the time spent travelling back and forth.

+++++++++

For six months, Ryan's parents used to bring him daily to our Programs Division in the evening time. For six months without any gaps, Ryan enjoyed a series of action videos in the audio-video hall of the Programs Division, on a big display screen for one hour per day. But the themes of those videos were different. In every video, every character would speak softly and only decent words would be spoken by the characters. In the guise of action movies, Ryan was shown practical moral lessons, step by step. There would be knives, like in the action movies, but those would not harm anyone, as they would be made of choco-vanilla. The music and the sound effects, the beats and rhythms, would be soothing and pleasant!

Every action would be prompt and full of suspense, even though there would not be any scenes of the fight, but so many interesting and lovely rhythmic jumps and dance sequences. Guns would not be pointed at any person but would be pointed at putting manure at the roots of the flower plants and spraying natural fragrances so that the most beautiful flowers could blossom in the hearts as well as on the ground and spread the message of love and peace.

+++++++++

Initially, for a couple of days, Ryan badly insisted on seeing the usual action movies that he used to see regularly at his residence, every day, in the afternoon, after coming back from school, as he was habitual to all of those. As his straight demand was not fulfilled, he began to make a ruckus for at least half an hour. But, after a few days, even without getting access to those movies, he used to spend the allotted one hour every day at the audio-video hall, as the sound quality, surrounding sound, sitting arrangement, color combination of the walls, the design of the false ceiling, and the overall ambiance of our hall were liked by Ryan so much. His parents made the provision that at home and at his friends' places he could no longer see any of the usual action, thriller, or horror movies.

If drops of water hit hard stone pieces repeatedly, the pieces will eventually decay. Similar things had happened with Ryan. Throughout the years, he had seen action movies with so many fights and gunshots. Surprisingly, after he completed one week at our Programs Division, he no longer demanded such movies. We tried to deeply enter his mind and discovered that Ryan was originally an innocent and action-loving boy by nature. The themes he chose were objectionable actions that would cause harm to anybody's original nature. Every day he used to devote the remaining two hours with the motivational trainer and coach to taking practical moral lessons through stage dramas and creative games specially made for morale-boosting.

Ryan was able to obtain and maintain the tempo of his desired gradual transformation with so many marvellous persistent actions, reactions, and reflections in his mind, taking him away from rowdiness in a gradual way, by the end of six consecutive months at 3 hrs per day at the Programs Division, as well as by his parents' efforts to maintain a similar environment at home.

"We are highly grateful to you, Aarna. You have really done a wonderful job that we thought would be impossible. Surprisingly, our son is no longer a rowdy boy but a loving child. He still yell's, but in a gentler tone and not over trivial matters, and unlike in the past, he does nothing more than kick his classmates.

Every morning, Ryan's mom sends a fresh "Rose of Appreciation" to my e-mail, which I share with everyone in our team.

CHAPTER 14: From being "allergic to music" to being "warm receptive to music"

Rita was a 20-year old girl, with the rare nature of avoiding music. Everybody loves music. Even animals and trees do. It's said that suitable music can help to bloom a budding flower. So, apparently, not liking music seems to be an odd component of someone's nature.

"This song is from the fresh album of a newly released movie, Rita."

"Listen to the tune; you will enjoy it."

Her new boyfriend, Ronit, would often tell her while taking her for a weekend drive.

"No Ronit, please make it off. I am not interested in listening."

Ronit would simply be obedient to what his girlfriend would request or demand and would turn the car stereo off without any objection and with lots of patience.

She would often make Ronit's mood off momentarily by coming out of the restaurants suddenly, at the time when food was about to be served by the waiter on the plates that he planned to enjoy with his girlfriend in candlelight. Such undesirable things happened only because of the reason that the background music from a conventional album or a live song was running inside, despite her request to turn it off.

However, Ronit was a boy who was always hopeful of getting a sunny dawn after dusk. So, he did not get disheartened at those happenings.

Her mother brought her to our office with the great hope that, like other cases, for her also, we would initiate some activities so that there could be at least some improvement in her non-compromising notion of "living without music."

"Any conventional popular music played in a car or in our house will be abruptly stopped by her; she is not patient enough to continue listening even for a moment. While on vacation, she does not allow us to keep the music system in the car on. But, everyone, except her, in our house is a music lover."

I could guess how frustrated her mom was after so many failed efforts to make her listen to the music that all others would happily enjoy.

Our team, including Om and I, had spent half an hour separately with Rita, her mom, and her boyfriend, Ronit. We had noted down all the points that we had observed. Finally, we developed a programme for Rita, in line with the recommendation of my papa, for a similar case (Case No. 624, Diary Number 6 of Papa).

However, my initial perspective about Rita changed dramatically after I interacted with her face-to-face, continuously for around half an hour. It was astonishing to know that, contrary to everyone's perspective about her 'allergy to music', she was, in fact, a deep lover of music; but, only the music of her choice. The usual and conventional music numbers did not attract her at all; they entered her eardrums as noises; so, they usually used to cause a headache for her. So, she used to avoid those strictly. The instrumental music of flute and sitar was her love, which she could plunge into and would enjoy listening to hours after hours, with non-diminishing attention and interest. She also liked the chirping of birds, the sound of waterfalls, the air wind, and the musical fountains.

The only issue was the difference in the choices, about which her mom and the other members of her family did not understand or did not try to understand. In fact, prior to her interactions with us, she did not open up at all with others about her choices in music, even after so many odd situations that were caused by the differences in choices.

Tussles used to arise frequently when the sensitive matter of music could not be handled in a cool way by the members of her house. Her intolerance and undesirable, abrupt reactions out of her bad temper were the parts of her autistic behaviors. However, her case could have been resolved in her family, with little understanding of her needs.

"Every time the situation in our house becomes so argumentative and awkward, I realize that I have not yet had the opportunity to open up. And even though my boyfriend maintains cool, he has never shown any interest in knowing about my musical choices."

Rita tried to put her points. But, I still feel that she could have found an opportunity to volunteer to open up, at least with her family, at some moment in the past.

"Rita will be coming to the audio-video hall of our Programs Division for two hours every day for the next four weeks."

I verbally informed her mom, on behalf of the Programs Division, and explained the plan in detail before handing over the plan sheet that we prepared for Rita. That plan was acceptable to her mom, as she was desperately waiting to get the problem of her daughter solved.

Every day, at our Programs Division, at her allotted time slot, Rita used to go through a music package consisting of a suitable blend of music, starting with her favorite flute piece and then with her all-time favorite sitar piece. Alternately, she used to enjoy the best flute and sitar albums. But, in between, some mixed numbers of diverse music were placed for small durations, with the extreme care that such inclusion would not be intolerable for her. In the first three days, she used to stop the music system as soon as a popular number was started, even though she started with very popular numbers. But, gradually, her resistance level came down, and by the end of her first week, she stopped resisting the popular numbers of our specially designed blended music packages.

The same girl, with complete intolerance of listening to the usual music, got used to listening to the homogeneous blends of music at our Audio-Video Hall.

Our team members took the joy of putting their smart efforts into developing the blends, especially for her, with lots of ideas and brilliance.

After every 15 minutes of flute play, there would be a popular song for 3 minutes. Then sitar plays for 15 minutes, and after that, another popular number for 3 minutes, and so on for around two hours. The contrast of the bass, rhythm, melody, texture, volume were so nicely matched by our associated musicians that nobody would be able to leave the Audio-Video Hall in between or after starting a musical session. That miraculously worked with Rita.

But, in that process, one more development happened. From some of her friends, she came to know about my inspiring music albums. She searched and picked up some top motivational albums of mine. She took the extension of another two weeks at 2 hours per day to listen to 29 of my music albums. When I came to her to assess the status, she hugged me and looked at my face with all admiration.

"Aarna, I just love your music albums. Those are so deep and soothing that people who have been awake for a long time will fall asleep; anyone planning to harm another in anger or for the purpose of retaliation will drop his or her weapons and cry out of regret, kneeling with folded hands to apologize for the wicked plan they have adopted! Your music has the power to naturally alleviate the devastating stresses and frustrations of life. I have become a big fan of your music, Ma'am...."

She kept on praising me. Her mom, siblings, friends and neighbors were all in the dark that she was a unique kind of music lover. But, actually, she was one of the few who could achieve such a high level of immersion in classical instrumental music through lots of dedication and exploration.

+++++++++

After six weeks of powerful daily sessions, there were many changes in Rita's behavior. By that time, she could at least bear any music number, not in the list of her favorites.

"Long years of built-in habits cannot be changed in six weeks; but, we need to be really happy due to some unbelievable visible changes in Rita, towards betterment."

"Thank you, Aarna, for doing so much for our daughter and for all of us!"

+++++++++

All the members of our team work very hard and with full dedication. So, they become very happy by seeing such good developments and by the feeling of completion of well-planned assignments to help someone get a better life.

CHAPTER 15: Transformation from the state of "Remaining fearful all the time due to negative approach" to "Remaining confident and courageous all the time due to positive approach."

At age 6, Jay, an autistic child, used to remain fearful all the time due to the wild imagination of the negative outcomes. He would not move on the staircase with the thought that he would miss the next step and would fall down. He would not cross the road with either of his parents, even at the zebra crossing, for fear that some car would start running suddenly and would hit them. In the past, his father had tried many times to lift him up to a great height, holding him with both hands. Parents usually play that way, and children usually enjoy the great heights without any fear. But Jay would always shout loudly out of fear of falling down. During festive seasons, he would nicely attend all the rehearsals prior to the stage shows. But, during the actual show on the stage, he would start crying so badly that his parents would have to take him down from the stage.

After preparing the list of all the observed and probable situations, we got the resemblance of a case described by Papa in Diary Number 2 (Case Number 228). The action team members sat for a discussion session based on Papa's recommendation. For all the situations leading to the imaginary phobia in the minds of children, Papa's recommendation was: "Let the child or adult face situations in which the imagined outcomes will be dreadful but will actually be very simple, with a very small chance of having any fearful effect.." All the members came to the conclusion that Papa's recommendation could be applied to Jay's case.

"From next Monday onwards, please bring Jay to our Programs Division every day for the next 30 days at 2 hours per day."

Our team had to work day and night to get the visuals ready for Jay at the earliest possible time, with the help of our contractual graphic designers. By the following Sunday, just prior to the start of Jay's improvement program, the visuals were prepared and tested.

Jay completed his 30 days of the improvement program. His father provided feedback on his child's situation. All the members of our action team sat together again on Jay's case. As the progress of the improvements in Jay's case was slow, we recommended an extension of his improvement programme duration for another two months without any gap.

"We have definitely seen some positive signs in him. So, please go ahead. Thank you so much for making so many good efforts for our son." His parents gladly gave the go-ahead for the proposed extension of his improvement program.

Jay's daily improvement session kept on running. Our team continued making new visuals with the help of the chosen graphic designers. Jay's positive responses to those visuals were quite encouraging for our determined team as well as for his parents.

By the end of three consecutive quality months of his program, Jay had developed lots of courage in him and was able to face and beat his imaginary phobias. Our team prepared visuals for 92 different cases related to imaginary phobias. We were going ahead with full dedication and with a "Never Give Up" attitude.

In one visual show, a boy would approach a staircase with his father. By looking at the visual, Jay shouted, "Stop him, stop him, he will have a big fall."

But, the boy did not fall down. His father held his hand and he climbed up the staircase step by step, easily and comfortably.

In another visual show, another boy would cross a road through the zebra crossing along with his mom when the green signal was on. While seeing the visual, Jay again shouted, "Stop him and his mom. Some car will hit them. "

But, the boy safely crossed the road while the green signal was on.

In another visual show, a boy of four would be lifted high by his father with both hands. While seeing the visual show, Jay shouted badly, "Stop, stop, stop; the boy will fall down."

But, the boy enjoyed the ride fearlessly and did not fall down.

The 92 short but distinct visual shows prepared by our team made a beautiful mark in the minds of Jay.

By the end of 92 days (2 hours per day), Jay had already transformed from a "fearful boy, with negativity in every step" to a "confident and courageous boy, with a positive approach."

CHAPTER 16: Transformation of a depressed girl with all-time suicidal thoughts into a highly ambitious girl with strong determination to achieve a high vision in life.

Eliana was a pretty girl at 14 with an inclination for fashion design. She was the only daughter of her highly educated, busy-working parents. In her early childhood, she was very jolly, having lots of fun with everyone. But, with time, so many changes came to her.

"She is in depression and, even at such an age, often talks about committing suicide. We are very worried. We took her to a renowned psychiatrist, and she is on medication. We love her a lot but are probably not able to provide her with the care she needs. Kindly help her regain her yesteryear's happiness. "

Her mom started weeping during her first one-on-one session with me.

"Do not worry, Madam. We will try our best. I hope everything will be fine."

Our team talked to Eliana separately. She was too emotional due to so many small issues.

"My Mammy and Papa badly neglect me. They love their jobs, take good care of their laptops and are concerned about their own needs. I have so many things to discuss with them; but, they are never free and are busy with meetings and meetings... "

While talking with her, we felt that she had so many complaints about her parents. However, her parents worked hard in their professional lives so that they could invest in her safer future and ensure that she would not face financial constraints in her future education and preparation for the specialized career of her choice.

We, all the members of the action team, sat together. Papa had noted down one similar incident in his diary number 4 (Case number 405). We brainstormed around his recommendation.

Finally, we prepared a three-month improvement plan for her, on a war footing, so that her improvement programme could be started without further delay, as the case was very delicate.

"From tomorrow onwards, please bring her to the Programs Division, every day for two hours, for the next three months." On behalf of the Foundation, I conveyed that to her parents.

Her parents happily agreed to our proposal and completed all the formalities of our Foundation, required to start her program.

+++++++++

For three months, Eliana was with us. Every day, she would attend one hour of motivational speech, listen to my motivational music for half an hour, and be in virtual reality for another half an hour, in which she would travel through the peaceful sky, wide sea with gentle waves, dazzling greenery, and beautiful flowers. Every day, her heart would be cherished with tranquilly and peace.

"We will be extremely careful that after completion of her improvement program, every day she can listen to at least one motivational speech, one motivational music album of yours, and inspiring videos of marvelous nature, sitting in her own room. We have already renovated her room as per her liking, with the help of an interior designer. We will let her feel that there is an abundance of love from our end."

Her parents conveyed enthusiastically to us their preparation in the middle of her improvement programme.

At the end of the three-month improvement programme, Eliana was a changed person. Her misunderstanding of her parents vanished; she returned to her goal of being a global-level fashion designer.

"I love the sky, the sea, the beautiful nature, my parents, all the people, and myself. I want to be a global level fashion designer and aspire to design the most beautiful, health-friendly outfits for everyone, from children to 100-year-old people. I have the dream that my designs will be loved by all the peoples of the earth."

She told me on the last day, at the concluding meeting at our office.

"Thank you so much, Aarna, for your generous help! You are really rendering great service through your foundation as well as through your inspiring music. May you be blessed always."

Eliana's parents were so happy to find their daughter in a motivated state and with a changed outlook on life.

+++++++++

In the last two and a half years, so many autistic children, adolescents, and adults have visited our Foundation Office. And the positive flow of hope continues flawlessly. They have all gone through their scheduled improvement programmes, designed and implemented by our team, based on Papa's recommendations.

The autistic people who visited our office came with their parents, relatives, or friends. My thoughts kept returning to those destitute and orphaned autistic children, who have no one to nourish them as they grow. Many times, my mind started traveling in different directions to find a way for those children.

One foggy morning with a shivering cold, I devised a plan to build a home near our Foundation Campus for those destitute orphan children, many of whom would undoubtedly be gifted ones. I knew that that was a tough plan, but I was ready to go through the turbulence to help them. I have shared my plan with Papa and he has loved it and has also expressed his willingness to participate in the same.

"In my view, in the first phase, we can choose a few children after scrutinizing the hidden potentials. Allow them to go through their respective improvement programmes and then nourish them. In the next phases, we can choose another few, and so on." That was Papa's suggestion.

+++++++++

There are five full-fledged qualified doctors and a couple of psychologists, who, in a team, manage everything, including welcoming the new visitors, taking fresh sessions with the newly visited autistic children or adults, making the materials and visuals ready for a new participant, and so many activities. Papa's diaries are our guidelines, as we have been able to find at least one case in his written notes that can be matched with every current new case of some autistic child or adult. Papa's intelligent recommendation for every case has been thoroughly analyzed and has been re-discovered as brilliantly superb, which has become the basis for designing and developing the improvement programmes for the autistic people that visit our Foundation Office.

"It's so nice to see the progress of your work, child. Really well done. Keep it up. It's good to know that you, Om, and your whole team have been working so diligently and dedicatedly for such a good cause. I am so happy that you have found some of my observations useful for your research and are able to successfully utilize some of them. I will keep on handing over all my new diaries to your foundation. "

This is one of Papa's recent messages to me. He means what he writes. Our whole action team is highly motivated by the grand gestures of my papa.

Papa is currently stationed at an R & D lab that is 6,000 km away from where Om & I stay. He is too busy developing an innovative, environmentally friendly product from the concept stage for his current organization. But, every day, at a mutually convenient time, we have at least one video chat on the strategy part of our foundation. The belief that has been ingrained in the mind of Papa by his micro-analysis of so many real-life cases is that every living character can actually do a miracle towards the better and from "the better" to "the best" if impelled to act in the right direction.

CHAPTER 17: Positive changes in my mom

Since my marriage with Om, my mom has got two homes: one that belongs to Papa and the other one that Om and I bought. My mom prefers to stay in our old house. But, whenever Papa is away, I pick her up at our house prior to Papa's departure to the airport. Since the time I was a child, there have been lots of changes in the behaviors and approaches of Mammy. That actually happened due to the improvements in my behaviors and status. With the close and consistent mentorship of my papa, many undesirable and abnormal behaviors in Mammy could be removed, slowly and steadily. She no longer nags others, bangs her head, or gossips with her neighbors about her daughter and husband.

"She has developed herself so much! And has overcome her situation with so much positive attitude and effort! Nowadays, every day, from all sides, I hear good things about her. Through her perseverance and ability, she has raised herself to the status of a celebrity musician. Her Foundation has got such a good name because of the selfless services she provides! We are so proud of her!" My Mammy made a brilliant speech, as per the request of the organizer, at the recent launch event of one of my music albums.

My mom served one big organization for 26 years as an accountant and took a voluntary retirement after her head surgery.

"Mammy, would you be interested in handling the Accounts Department of our Foundation?" I knew that she would happily agree, as she loved her job in accounting.

"It will be my pleasure, child."

Since then, my mom has been handling all the accounting functions of our Foundation, as the CFO (Chief Financial Officer). Professionalism has its own place. Mammy's professionalism, expertise, and sincerity as the CFO are at the optimum level. Papa has appreciated my choice for the position of CFO.

She would request documented proof of each and every expense from all departments before entering into the relevant record files. She always maintains the latest records of how much money is transferred every month to our Foundation's account from my royalty income, from my rewards and the stage shows, and from Papa's account. She would not allow any financial issues to remain in the pending state. Mammy has been enjoying her post-retirement job and is very happy. We have been paying a good salary to her every month on time, to pay her due regard for her experience, expertise, and sincerity. Her selection and joining as the CFO was one of the best events for our Foundation.

+++++++++

Interestingly, my interactions with Mammy on our Foundation's financial matters remain limited to her formal office hours, 9 am to 6 pm.

From Monday to Saturday every week, beyond the office hours, and on Sunday, she is strictly my Mammy only and nobody else.

I used to see her gloomy face every day during my childhood and adolescence; nowadays, she keeps smiling all the time. Earlier, she used to nag me all the time; nowadays, her sentences are full of unlimited praise for me. Earlier, she used to speak very roughly; nowadays, she speaks very smoothly and gently.

With the slow and gradual stages of transformation in the last so many years, my mammy has transformed from being a restless mother with no tolerance for any deviation to a cool lady with a balanced temperament. After talking to her, even for hours, nobody would make out that she was the same lady who used to cause a ruckus in our house and bang her head multiple times a month on petty matters.

CHAPTER 18: Transformation from "an autistic girl, apparently most deficient in all aspects" to "an inspiring musician with millions of followers and a determined worker for the global social cause of helping autistic children, adolescents and adults"

"Never Give Up; Never Say Die" is one of the strong principles that has been deep-rooted in my mind by my papa, through his consistent efforts throughout the years. In my childhood and adolescence, I happened to be almost broke internally; every time I would start something, people would start bullying and teasing me because I would keep mum in groups; my face would look serious all the time in public places, even though I wanted to smile openly; people would gaze at me and would make fun of me when I would walk as if they were waiting to see some strange funny item. People would mark me as mentally ill and would walk away from my vicinity, making me lonely whereas I wanted to be with them.

To my papa, I was the most intelligent girl in my class. He used to keep on motivating me to take the challenge to win over the odds. Every single day was a challenge for me to get over the deficiencies that became the points for getting ridiculed. In reality, I worked the hardest and the smartest, crossing all the limits to overcome my initial status. When everyone around me, including my mother, lost hope in me, I began to see the light at the end of my gloomy days. Papa kept on nurturing me most diligently, through his wonderful paternal love, holding my hands and guiding me while taking every forward leap. During those days, Papa actually brightened my hope by showing me how my vision could be so clear and high that I could get my thoughts and actions elevated to a great height in terms of grandeur and enlightenment.

+++++++++

The exclusive works on my music are the ongoing activities that I do most diligently, without interruption, after returning from the Foundation Office, unless I am late from some stage music show or music video launch or award receiving or felicitation event.

The hands of the clocks on the walls of all the rooms of our house are running at the same speed and rhythm, so, even though the movements of the hands in the clocks are monotonous, the accuracy, alertness, and dynamism of the clocks motivate me every day to keep going. We need to accomplish so many value-added activities every day, in 24 hours. We are bound to follow the timeline strictly, every single day, and have found the amazing result of the same.

To facilitate better concentration on the ongoing activities and their smooth succession, Om and I need to keep on blocking the waste of memory, thoughts, and imagination every now and then, so that no non-value-added activity can dampen our purpose and energy. Even after being fully engaged at the Foundation Office for 10 hours every day, including Sundays, we both remain energetic all day long by adhering to six warm-up breaks of 10 minutes each.

+++++++++

In the background of my mind, the process of creation of the new tunes keeps on running continuously, 24 x 7, without causing any disturbance in the speed or performance of the ongoing activities. That's why, every late evening, I devote the whole three hours to developing the tune that was already created in my mind and was looking for a suitable medium.

+++++++++

The path chosen by me, under the mentorship of Papa, has been full of challenges where consistent efforts and repeated mental impulsions are required to remain on track. I was diagnosed with autism. But I dared to imagine myself in a position where I could create music that would touch millions of hearts and also be a part of a global movement to help autistic children, adolescents, and adults live the dignified lives they deserve in the best way possible.

Due to my strong aspiration, I let myself perspire as much as I could and am still continuing to improve my status, to get stronger to help all those with similar pains in getting dignified status. Due to my challenge to win, I started becoming the main vocal instead of remaining dumb in every group that I joined. As soon as I entered my college for graduation, people started seeing my smiling face all the time instead of my serious look of yesteryear; so many people, including those who used to make fun of the way I used to walk, started following my confident way of walking!

But, all those things did not happen miraculously. In fact, nothing happens miraculously. Only Papa and I have been witnessing the struggles of my gradual changes, bit by bit. For every matter, once the matter is picked up for improvement, we both plan meticulously.

Papa has taught me how to speak effectively; which letters and words to give more stress; where the tongue should touch for every spoken letter; how much eyes need to be opened for each expression; how to maintain the natural smile in the eyes, while speaking in front of someone; how the lips movements should be, while speaking different sentences; while speaking, where to take halt to give chance to others to reply or comment; how to move and tilt the neck, head, hands, fingers and feet while delivering speech; how to maintain voice modulation, while expressing different feelings. My papa taught me all those, step by step, with exceptional patience, onsite as well as online, depending on his availability. He would teach and repeat, and then give me assignments to complete. I had to stand and sit in front of the giant mirror in my room and do my practice hours after hours. Papa would wait until there would be sufficient improvement in a particular step before going ahead to the next one. Nobody else, except me, knows how many sleepless nights I had spent practicing the steps to get Papa's approval to be eligible for the next step.

To complete all the steps of speaking effectively, it probably took me one and a half years without any gaps, and Papa kept on teaching without losing patience, all day long, either online or onsite, even though the majority of the time he used to stay out of station. He repeatedly reminded me to practise even after I had mastered a step.

My training on how to walk and stand for different occasions was started by Papa after I completed his long training on speaking. Walking on the passenger's pathway and on the stage while delivering a speech or walking in a seminar in between the rows of chairs with people sitting on those—all were distinct.

"My dear child, whatever may be the occasion, your speech or walk or standing posture reflects your confidence level." For more than six months, Papa taught me how to walk and stand on different occasions. The agony and the hunger to win over the deficiencies kept me moving. Even though improvements do not have a definite measure, I used to feel how much I improved every single day.

In college, during my undergrad, graduation, and post-grad studies, I kept on applying whatever I learned from Papa, while talking, walking, and standing. The results were wonderful. I started to become a lovable friend to everyone, with a natural spontaneity.

"Keep on chasing your role models, child. Observe each of their movements and follow the practices that make you feel gorgeous. I have learned some of the good practices of talking, walking, and grooming that way and am still learning." That was one of the secrets of his success that he shared with me when I first started college, and it inspired me to work hard and make the necessary changes in myself.

+++++++++

As per my experience, autism eventually is a boon. These children are blessed with extraordinary skills and capabilities. The path I have chosen is the one not generally aspired to and targeted by people. The majority give up before half-way, out of desperation.

+++++++++

Every month, Papa donates 60% of his salary to the account of The Boundless Ambit Foundation, founded by him. He handed over the foundation to me due to his confidence in my hard work and sincerity. When I started earning my royalty income from my music albums and stage shows, I started following the path of Papa by donating 80% of my royalty income and stage show earnings to the Foundation Account. That got increased to 90% after Om's assurance and encouragement.

All the expenses of the Foundation Campus, including the building construction, renovation, and maintenance; setting and maintaining the pathways; the cost of running the improvement programs; the administrative costs; and all other costs are covered by the money donated by Papa and me.

My relatives and some close friends keep on making remarks on the matter of the 90% donation of my income as "too generous".

"You could have kept at least 50% of your income to have a luxurious life." That is the suggestion of many people. I think, my definition of luxury is different from that of the majority.

I can feel real comfort, enjoyment, delight, and satisfaction through the act of donation. So, I can say that I am living a luxurious life by maintaining genuine happiness and continuing to earn by donating my hard-earned income for a noble cause. It gives me tremendous peace and joy to express my way of defining luxury.

+++++++++

There are lakhs of autistic people in the world, and every year, so many autistic babies are born. I have the dream that, on successful completion of our research project, many people will be able to start seeing autism as a boon.

+++++++++

Papa has recently expressed his plan to start writing the story of my life that he is planning to publish with the title "Her Unbounded Leaps: An Inspiring Novel of Winning."

"My dear child, I am sure your eventful story will inspire everybody, irrespective of location, class, creed, and religion." Papa has shared his plan with me a number of times.

I am so honored with the most recent gesture from my beloved papa!

For me, life with the sense and the ability to handle the responsibility for the wellbeing of the world has just begun, at the age of 25.

And, at the age of 55, my papa thinks generously that his life has begun to dedicatedly contribute to the wellbeing of the world.

www.ingramcontent.com/pod-product-compliance
Lightning Source LLC
LaVergne TN
LVHW100200061126
851857LV00010B/336
* 9 7 9 8 2 1 5 9 8 3 7 1 3 *